Lives and Times

Stephen Foster

The Man Behind our Best-Loved Songs

Peggy Pancella

Heinemann Library
Chicago, Illinois

Designed by Lucy Owen and Bridge Creative Services
Originated by Modern Age Repro
Printed and bound by South China Printing Company

10 09 08 07 06
10 9 8 7 6 5 4 3 2 1

Library of Congress Cataloging-in-Publication Data
Pancella, Peggy.
   Stephen Foster / Peggy Pancella.
      p. cm. -- (Lives and times)
   Includes bibliographical references and index.
   ISBN 1-4034-6748-X (library binding-hardcover)
   1. Foster, Stephen Collins, 1826-1864--Juvenile
literature. 2. Composers--United States--Biography--
Juvenile literature. I. Title. II. Series: Lives and times
(Des Plaines, Ill.)
   ML3930.F6P36 2005
   782.42164'092--dc22
                                    2005001496

Acknowledgments
The author and publishers are grateful to the following
for permission to reproduce copyright material:
Corbis/Bettmann pp. **4, 9, 18, 22**; Corbis/Kevin R.
Morris p. **21**; Corbis/Museum of the City of New York
p. **16**; Corbis/Raymond Gehman pp. **26, 27**; Lebrecht
Music Collection p. **5**; Library of Congress p. **11**;
Rosalind Hudson p. **8**; Stephen Foster Archive pp. **6, 7,
10, 12, 13, 14, 15, 19a, 19b, 20, 23, 24, 25**;
The Bridgeman Art Library/New York Historical
Society p. **17**.

Cover photograph of Stephen Foster reproduced with
permission of Corbis. Photograph of music manuscript
reproduced with permission of Corbis.

Page icons by Creatas/Brand X

Photo research by Maria Joannou and Virginia
Stroud-Lewis

Every effort has been made to contact copyright
holders of any material reproduced in this book.
Any omissions will be rectified in subsequent
printings if notice is given to the publishers.

Contents

Some words are shown in bold, **like this**. You can find out what they mean by looking in the glossary.

Introducing Stephen Foster

Stephen Foster was a **musician** and **composer**. He wrote more than 200 pieces of music. His tunes became very popular. Many of them are still well known.

Stephen's songs had simple tunes and words. They were easy for people to understand.

When Stephen was alive, people in the United States were not all equal. Some—especially African Americans—worked for others as **slaves**. Many of Stephen's songs sound like the music these workers used to sing.

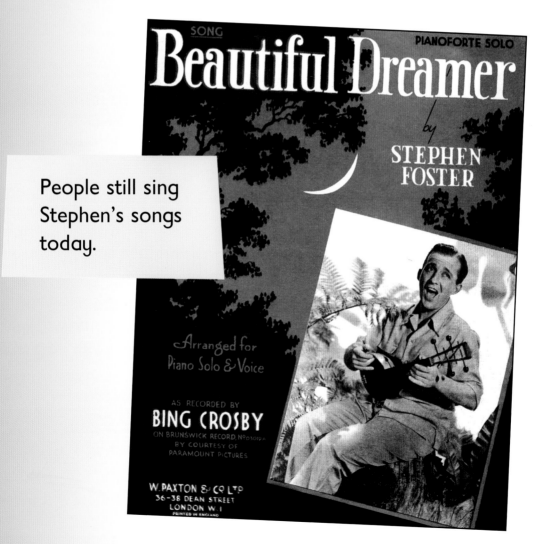

People still sing Stephen's songs today.

Little Stephy

Stephen was born in Lawrenceville, Pennsylvania, on July 4, 1826. There were eleven children in his family, but three of them died young. Little Stephy grew up as the baby of the family.

Stephen was born in this house, called the White Cottage.

Stephen's parents helped to set up the town of Lawrenceville. It is near Pittsburgh.

Stephen's family liked to make music together. His father played the violin. His sisters played piano and guitar. Stephen first tried his sister's guitar when he was two years old.

Early Learning

Stephen started school when he was five. He did not like to study. He wanted to quit school. His older sister taught him at home for a while. Later he went to other schools and did much better work.

Stephen was very smart, but school bored him. He liked to be alone with his thoughts.

8

Sometimes Stephen watched workers loading and unloading boats along the river. He liked the songs they sang.

Stephen liked music better than school. His father thought studying music was a waste of time, but Stephen did not stop. Listening to people singing and playing helped him learn many new kinds of songs.

A Gift for Music

Stephen often amazed people with his **talent**. When he was seven, he visited a music store and picked up a **flageolet**. He had never used one before. But in just a few minutes, he played a whole tune.

This was Stephen's flageolet. He later learned to play the flute, too.

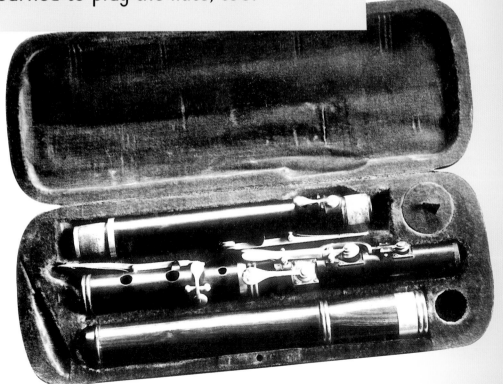

Stephen also loved to watch **minstrel** shows at the theater. Then he and his friends put on their own shows. Stephen was usually the star. He sang and danced just like the real performers did.

Minstrels sang, danced, and told jokes. People enjoyed their funny shows.

Comings and Goings

When Stephen was young, his father's business failed. The family moved to Allegheny, Pennsylvania. Stephen brought along his **flageolet**. He tried to learn piano and guitar, too.

Stephen wrote this letter to his father in 1837. He was ten and a half years old.

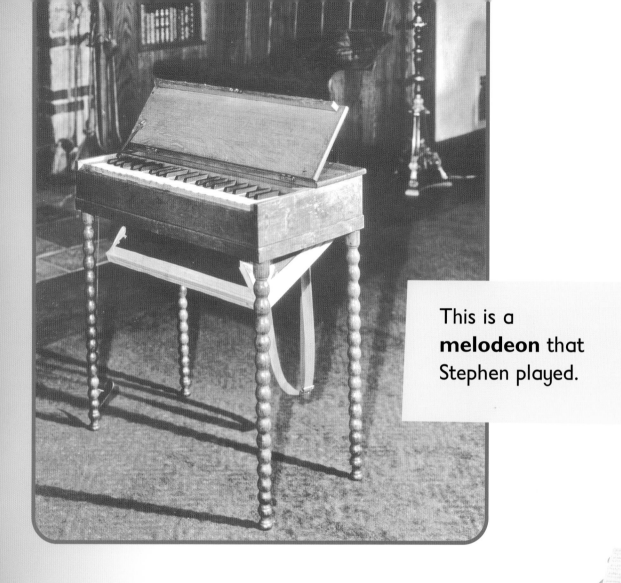

This is a **melodeon** that Stephen played.

Stephen's family also visited his uncle's farm in Poland, Ohio. Stephen loved being free to do what he wanted there. Once they stayed for almost a year. Then he went away to school in a nearby town.

A Real Composer

Stephen did not like his new school much. He missed his family and his home. But he **composed** his first piece of music there. It was called the "Tioga **Waltz**."

Henry Kleber gave Stephen piano lessons. He also helped Stephen compose some of his music.

Stephen wrote the music for "Open Thy Lattice, Love." Someone else wrote the words.

The next year Stephen returned home to work on his music. He was still a teenager when he wrote "Open Thy **Lattice**, Love." This was the first song he ever **published**.

New Work

Stephen did not make much money writing songs. He needed a steady job. So he went to Cincinnati, Ohio, to work for his brother as a **bookkeeper**. Stephen thought it was dull, but he did a good job.

Stephen rode a **steamboat** to Cincinnati. His office was near the Ohio River.

Stephen still **composed** music, too.
He entered song contests and won prizes.
Songs like "Oh! Susanna" and "Camptown
Races" became popular. People liked the
funny words and **catchy** tunes.

Many of Stephen's music ideas
came from **folk songs** and tunes
he heard workers singing.

A Family of His Own

Stephen's music became more and more popular. He wrote and **published** many new songs. Soon he was earning a good living from his music. He quit his office job and returned home to Pittsburgh.

There were lots of factories in Pittsburgh.

These pictures show Stephen's wife Jane (left) and their daughter Marion (below).

Stephen fell in love with an old friend named Jane McDowell. They were married in 1850. Their only daughter, Marion, was born the next year.

Happy Times

Stephen wanted his family to have many good times. They often saw shows at theaters. Marion took dancing lessons and went to parties. Stephen also let her watch quietly while he **composed** music.

These are notes Stephen made when he was writing "Old Folks at Home."

Some think "My Old Kentucky Home" is about this house, called Federal Hill. Friends of Stephen's lived here.

Many of the songs Stephen wrote during this time have become famous, such as "My Old Kentucky Home" and "Old Folks at Home." Their words show how much the idea of home meant to Stephen.

Life Changes

In 1853 Stephen moved to New York. He worked for the company that **published** much of his music. Jane and Marion stayed at home. Stephen hoped to earn enough money to bring them to New York as well.

This is what New York looked like at the time Stephen moved there.

After about a year, Stephen felt homesick. He returned to his family. But soon his mother died, followed by his father. Stephen was very sad. He stayed home for several years, until his money ran low again.

This is Stephen (on the left) with George Cooper. George wrote words for some of Stephen's songs.

A Lonely Ending

Stephen returned to New York with his family in 1860. But soon Jane and Marion moved back home. The country also went to war. Stephen felt lonely and upset. He wrote many sad songs.

This picture shows how Stephen looked late in life.

Stephen had only 38 cents in his wallet when he died. The paper scrap shows his idea for a new song.

Early in 1864 Stephen grew ill. One day he fell and cut himself on a **washbasin**. He was taken to a hospital, where he died on January 13. He was only 37 years old.

The Music Goes On

Stephen always loved his family and his home. So he was buried in Pittsburgh, near his parents' graves. Today there is a large museum about Stephen's life and music at the University of Pittsburgh.

This is the living room of the Federal Hill mansion in Bardstown, Kentucky.

This is a statue of Stephen in the My Old Kentucky Home State Park in Bardstown.

Stephen's music is still performed today. The words are old-fashioned, but they tell about ideas that are still important. Some pieces have been used on TV or in movies. People love to hear the **catchy** tunes.

27

Fact File

- The day Stephen was born was special in the United States. The country had begun exactly 50 years earlier. Stephen's father missed his son's birth because he was at a big celebration in town.

- Stephen's songs were very popular, but he never made very much money from them. He often charged very low prices when he sold his songs.

- "Oh! Susanna" was Stephen's first big hit. He **published** it in 1848. It soon became famous across the country. It has even been changed into other languages.

- Two states chose Stephen's music for their state songs. Florida uses "Old Folks at Home" and Kentucky uses "My Old Kentucky Home."

Timeline

1826 Stephen Foster is born in Lawrenceville, Pennsylvania, on July 4

1831 Stephen begins school

1841 Stephen writes the "Tioga **Waltz**"

1844 Stephen's first song—"Open Thy **Lattice**, Love"—is published

1846 Stephen goes to work for his brother in Cincinnati, Ohio

1850 Stephen moves back home; he marries Jane McDowell

1851 Stephen's daughter, Marion, is born; he publishes "Old Folks at Home"

1853 Stephen publishes "My Old Kentucky Home"; he moves to New York

1854 Stephen moves home from New York

1855 Stephen's mother and father die

1860 Stephen's family moves back to New York

1864 Stephen dies on January 13

Glossary

bookkeeper person who keeps track of money for a business

catchy pleasing and easy to remember

compose to make up music

composer person who makes up music

flageolet small instrument like a flute which is played by blowing into it

folk song simple song shared by people from a certain country or area

lattice neat pattern of crossed wooden or metal strips, often used on a window, door, or gate

melodeon small keyboard instrument

minstrel person who performs certain styles of songs, dances, and jokes

musician person who makes music

publish have something printed so that it can be sold to other people

slave person who is forced to work as a servant for someone else

steamboat boat that gets power from steam

talent special gift or ability to do something well

waltz kind of dance music that has patterns of three beats

washbasin large bowl of water which is used to wash in

Find Out More

More Books to Read

An older reader can help you with these books:

Krull, Kathleen. *I Hear America Singing! Folksongs for American Families*. New York, N.Y.: Knopf Books, 2003.

Zannos, Susan. *The Life and Times of Stephen Foster*. Bear, Del.: Mitchell Lane, 2003.

Places to Visit

There are many places in the United States that honor Stephen Foster. They include:

My Old Kentucky Home State Park, Bardstown, Kentucky

Stephen Collins Foster Memorial Home, Pittsburgh, Pennsylvania

Stephen C. Foster State Park, Fargo, Georgia

Stephen Foster Folk Culture Center State Park, White Springs, Florida

Stephen Foster Memorial, Center for American Music, University of Pittsburgh, Pennsylvania

Tioga Point Museum, Athens, Pennsylvania.

Index